Homemade Soup Recipes:
Simple and Easy
Slow Cooker Recipes

Cathy L. Kidd

Table of Contents

Introduction

One of the advantages of making soup in your slow cooker is the richness of flavor from the slow cooking process. The other obvious advantage is the ease and convenience. Although some of the recipes in this book require some advance preparation of the ingredients, most are "dump them in and turn it on." You can put everything in your slow cooker in the morning and your soup will be ready when you get home for dinner.

Although we tend to think about soup in the cold winter months, these recipes make wonderful comfort meals any time of the year. Plus there are a couple recipes that can be served chilled for warm days.

To Stir or Not To Stir

Some recipes call for a careful mixing of the ingredients before cooking and others call for the ingredients to be layered and not stirred. The reasoning behind this is that some ingredients like uncooked meat, potatoes and carrots take longer to cook and do better if they are lower in the slow cooker closer to the heat source. Be sure to read the instructions carefully so you'll get the best results.

Brand Name Products

If product brand names are mentioned in the recipes, they are intended as guides for finding the ingredient in your store. Other options may be available depending on your local area. Don't feel obligated to purchase the brand name product in order to get perfect soup.

Adapting Stove Top Recipes

If you have a favorite stove top soup recipe, it can be successfully cooked in the slow cooker if you follow a few simple guidelines. You can also use similar recipes in this book as a guide when adapting one of your stove top recipes.

Liquids: Generally, the amount of liquid called for in a recipe can be decreased by about half. Monitor it every so often while cooking to be sure it doesn't boil over and there is enough liquid for the thickness of soup you like.

Pasta and Rice: When the recipe calls for cooked pasta, cook it according to package directions until almost done before adding it. This way it won't get mushy in the final soup. Most of the recipes will also suggest adding the cooked pasta and rice in the last stage of cooking. When using rice, it is most often best to pre-cook it a little before adding it so it will be cooked enough.

Dried Beans: Most of the recipes suggest soaking the beans overnight before cooking them in the slow cooker. To save time you can substitute canned beans but if you do the cooking time will no doubt need to be reduced.

Herbs and Spices: Ground herbs and spices lose their flavor over long cooking times, so it's best to add them near the end. Whole herbs release their flavors over time better, so they are a better choice. You should always taste and if necessary adjust the seasonings before serving.

Milk/Cheese: Milk, sour cream, and heavy cream break down over long cooking times. They should be added during the final stages of cooking. Condensed cream soups are good substitutions for milk and can be cooked longer. Cheeses don't generally hold up over long cooking times so they should be added near the end of cooking.

Vegetables: Dense vegetables like potatoes, carrots, and other root vegetables should be cut no larger than 1″ thick and placed in the bottom of the pot since they take longer to cook.

Substitutions
If you are concerned about fat or sodium in your diet, use fat free and reduced sodium broth and canned vegetables in the recipes that call for them. Reduced fat cream soups can also be used in any recipe as a substitute for the higher calorie version. Also, trim off any chicken or beef fat before cooking. Kitchen scissors make this an easy and fast process.

Chicken thighs are called for in many of the recipes because they keep their shape better and remain moist during the long cooking time. They also enhance the flavor of the soup more than chicken breasts. It's amazing how much of a difference the thighs make in the overall flavor of your soup! Boneless chicken thighs may be hard to find in your area. You can substitute thighs with the bone in, but you will need to remove the skin before placing them into the slow cooker and then remove them and shred the meat off the bone before the final cooking stage.

With some ingenuity, any of the recipes can be adapted for vegetarians. Obviously the vegetable based ones won't need much adjustment, but the ones calling for meat will. There are a number of "mock meat" products available now. Depending on the consistency of the product you may need to adjust the cooking time when you add it to the slow cooker. Other than that, let your imagination guide you!

Making Your Own Soup Stock and Broth

The slow cooker is perfect for making your own soup stock or broth. Just add the ingredients, set it to the low setting and let it cook overnight. When you make your own, you can control the flavor as well as the fat and sodium content. I've included the recipe to create chicken stock, one of the most common ingredients in this book.

Technically the difference between stock and broth is the bones. Stock is made with bones where a broth isn't. But you can easily strain the stock after cooking to get a clear broth.

You can adjust the recipe to make beef stock with beef bones instead of chicken and if you use vegetables only you'll have vegetable stock. Be sure to use the stock or broth within 2 days as it will start to lose flavor after that. It does not freeze well.

Your Slow Cooker

Slow cooker sizes vary from 1 1/2 to as much as 9 quarts. The most popular sizes are between 3 1/2 and 6 quarts. The one you already have will most likely be in that range. If you are not sure what size it is, a quick and easy way to find out is to add water and count how many cups it holds. Counting 4 cups to a quart will tell you what size slow cooker you have!

Because there are so many choices, the recipes in this book do not give suggestions on the size to use. In general the quantities are for the 6 quart size, so you may need to make adjustments to accommodate what you have. Slow cooker manufacturers generally recommend filling the pot half to three-quarters full so it doesn't boil over. Also if there are additional items that need to be added at the end of cooking, you'll need to keep that in mind when you measure your ingredients.

Another consideration is how large your family is and how many days you want to be eating the same soup! Most of these soups will freeze well so you can make extra and freeze it for another day when you have less time to cook.

If you adjust the quantities proportionally you won't go wrong. On the other hand, you can use more of the ingredients you especially like and leave out ones you don't care for. One of the beauties of slow cooker cooking is in its flexibility.

After cooking, cleaning your slow cooker can be a challenge. You'll want to let it cool, but I find if you can clean it while it's still warm, it is easier. You want to avoid using abrasive pads and use a sponge or rubber spatula instead to get off any residue on the sides.

Some of the newer models have a removable inner liner that can be put into the dishwasher. I find it's best to remove any residue first. It will come out cleaner.

The outside can be cleaned with a soft cloth and warm, soapy water but be sure not to completely immerse it in water.

With some care, your slow cooker will last for years, just like mine, pictured in this book. I can't tell you how old it is!

The Recipes

Almond Wild Rice Chicken Soup

2 tablespoons	Butter
1/2 cup	Dry wild rice
6 cups	Chicken broth
1/2 cup	Onion, minced
1/2 cup	Celery, chopped
2 cups	Chicken, cooked and chopped
1/2 cup	Slivered almonds, toasted

Place the butter into a small skillet over medium heat. Add the rice and sauté for 10 minutes. Remove the rice from the skillet and place it in the slow cooker. Pour in the chicken broth and stir. Add the onion and celery and stir to combine well. Cover the slow cooker and cook on the low setting for 4 hours.

Add the chicken and continue cooking on low for 1 hour.

Serve with the almonds sprinkled on the top.

Asparagus Soup

2 pounds	Fresh asparagus, ends removed, cut into 1" pieces
5 cups	Chicken broth
6	Green onions, finely chopped
2 cups	Baking potatoes, peeled, cubed
1/4 teaspoon	Seasoned salt
1/4 teaspoon	Ground pepper
	Fresh parsley, chopped

Rinse the asparagus and place in the slow cooker. Add the broth, green onions and potatoes. Cover and cook on the low setting for 5 to 7 hours or until the potatoes are tender.

Remove the vegetables and puree them in a blender with a little of the liquid, until somewhat smooth. Return to the slow cooker and stir in the salt and pepper. Cover and cook on the high setting for 30 minutes.

Serve with a few cooked asparagus tips or fresh parsley on top, if desired. A swirl of pureed roasted red pepper with sour cream would also make a colorful and flavorful topping.

Barbecue Bean Soup

1 pound	Great Northern beans, soaked
2 teaspoons	Salt
1 medium	Onion, chopped
1/8 teaspoon	Ground pepper
2 pounds	Beef short ribs
6 cups	Water
3/4 cup	Barbecue sauce

Place all of the ingredients in the slow cooker except the barbecue sauce. Cover and cook on the low setting 10 to 16 hours.

Before serving, remove the short ribs and cut the meat from the bones. Return the meat to the slow cooker. Stir in the barbecue sauce and heat thoroughly before serving.

Barley, Mushroom and Green Onion Soup

1 cup	Barley
1 (14 1/2 oz) can	Roasted garlic chicken broth (Swanson)
1/2 cup	Green onions, thinly sliced
4- 6 ounces	Fresh or canned mushrooms, sliced
	Salt or seasoned salt and pepper to taste
2 teaspoons	Butter or margarine

Combine all of the ingredients in the slow cooker. Cover and cook on the low setting for 4 to 4 1/2 hours.

Bayou Gumbo with Rice

3 tablespoons	All Purpose Flour
3 tablespoons	Oil
1/2 pound	Smoked sausage, cut into 1/2 inch slices
2 cups	Okra, cut
1 large	Onion, chopped
1 large	Green bell pepper, chopped
3 cloves	Garlic, minced
1/4 teaspoon	Ground red pepper (cayenne)
1/4 teaspoon	Black pepper
1 (14.5 oz.) can	Diced tomatoes, with liquid
1 (12 oz.) package	Medium shrimp, frozen cooked, shelled, deveined, rinsed
1 1/2 cups	Long-grain white rice, uncooked

In a small saucepan, combine the flour and oil and mix well. Cook over a medium high heat, stirring constantly for 5 minutes. Reduce the heat to medium and cook, stirring constantly, for about 10 minutes.

Place the flour-oil mixture in the slow cooker. Stir in all of the remaining ingredients except the shrimp and rice. Cover and cook on the low setting for 7 to 9 hours.

When ready to serve, cook the rice as directed on the package. Meanwhile, add the shrimp to the gumbo mixture in the slow cooker and mix well. Cover and cook on the low setting for an additional 20 minutes. Serve the gumbo over the rice.

16 Bean Soup

1 package	16 Bean Soup Mix (Goya)
3	Bay leaves
1 tablespoon	Oregano, crushed
2 cans	Chicken stock
	Additional water to cover
3 stalks	Celery, chopped
3	Carrots, diced
1 large	Onion, chopped
3 cloves	Garlic, sliced
1 pound	Turkey Italian sausage, sliced
2 cans	Stewed or diced tomatoes

Combine the first 5 ingredients (the liquid should cover the beans by 1-2") in the slow cooker. Cook on the high setting for 2 hours Add the remaining ingredients, turn the temperature to the low setting and cook for an additional 3 hours.

Serve as complete meal or over rice. Freezes well.

Note: For a more spicy soup, add some cayenne or crushed red pepper when adding the second set of ingredients.

Bean Soup Congressional Style

1 pound	Small white beans
8 cups	Water
2 cups	Ham, diced
1 cup	Onion, diced
1 cup	Celery, chopped
2 tablespoons	Parsley, chopped
1 teaspoon	Salt
1/4 teaspoon	Pepper
1	Bay leaf

Place the ingredients in the slow cooker. Cover and cook on the low setting for 8 to 10 hours or until the beans are tender. Remove the bay leaf before serving.

Bean Soup Hickory Smoked

3 cups	Cooked ham, cut into cubes
2 cups	Water
1 cup	Dried navy beans
1 cup	Celery, sliced
1 small	Onion, chopped
2	Carrots, sliced
1/4 teaspoon	Dried thyme
1/4 teaspoon	Liquid smoke
1/4 cup	Parsley, chopped

Place the ham into the slow cooker and pour the water over the top. Add the rest of the ingredients, except for the parsley, and stir to combine well. Cover and cook on the low setting for 10 hours.

Sprinkle the parsley over the top just before serving.

Note: Liquid smoke gives this soup an added taste and can be found in the condiment section of your grocery store.

Bean Soup with Short Ribs

1 pound	Great North Beans, soaked overnight, rinsed and drained
3/4 cup	Onion, chopped
1/8 teaspoon	Pepper
1 1/2 pounds	Beef short ribs
6 cups	Water
1 teaspoon	Salt
1 cup	Barbecue sauce

Place the soaked beans into the slow cooker. Add the onion and pepper. Place the short ribs on top and pour in the water. Stir gently. Cover and cook on the low setting for 10 hours.

Remove the short ribs and use two forks to shred the meat off the bones. Return the meat to the slow cooker and pour in the barbecue sauce. Cover and cook on the high setting for 30 minutes.

Note: If you'd like a little more of a beef taste replace one of the cups of water with 1 can of beef broth.

Beef Soup with Bow Tie Pasta

1 pound	Beef chuck, cut into cubes
2 (14.5 oz.) cans	Diced tomatoes with basil, garlic and oregano
2 (14 oz.) can	Beef broth
1 (15 oz.) can	Cannellini beans, rinsed and drained
1 (15 oz.) can	Kidney beans, rinsed and drained
1 cup	Carrots, sliced thin
1 small	Onion chopped
1/4 teaspoon	Salt
1/4 teaspoon	Pepper
1 cup	Bow tie pasta, uncooked
	Grated Parmesan cheese

Place the beef into the slow cooker. Add the tomatoes (including the juice) and broth. Stir in both types of beans. Add the carrots, onions, salt and pepper and stir well. Cover and cook on the low setting for 8 hours or on the high setting for 4 hours.

Stir in the uncooked pasta and continue cooking at the high setting for 40 minutes or until the pasta is tender.

Serve with a little grated Parmesan cheese on the top if desired.

Note: If you can't find diced tomatoes with the spices in your grocery store, you can get plain diced tomatoes and add the spices to taste.

Beef Soup with Cabbage

1/2 head	Cabbage, chopped
1 medium	Onion, chopped
1 large	Carrot, sliced
3-4 tablespoons	Cooked rice
2 ribs	Celery, sliced
1 teaspoon	Garlic powder
3 cups	Beef broth
1 pound	Soup bones or beef shanks
2 (14 1/2 oz.) cans	Diced tomatoes
	Salt and pepper to taste

Place all of the ingredients in the slow cooker in the order listed. Cover and cook on the low setting for 8 to 10 hours.

Beef, Beer and Vegetable Soup

3 medium	Onions, sliced
1 pound	Carrots, cut into 1/2" slices
4	Parsnips, cut into 1/2" slices
2	Bay leaves
4 cloves	Garlic, minced
1/2 teaspoon	Pepper
1 tablespoon	Fresh thyme, snipped or 1 teaspoon dried thyme, crushed
2 tablespoons	Quick cooking tapioca
1 1/2 pounds	Beef stew meat, cut into 1" cubes
1 (14 1/2 oz) can	Beef broth
1 (12 oz) can	Beer

Place the onions, carrots, parsnips, bay leaves, garlic, pepper and dried thyme (if you are using that) in the slow cooker. Sprinkle with the tapioca. Place the meat on top of the vegetables. Add beef broth and beer.

Cover and cook on the low setting for 10 to 12 hours or on the high setting for 5 to 6 hours.

Before serving, remove the bay leaves and if using fresh thyme instead of dried, stir it in now.

Note: You can use non alcoholic beer if you like.

Beef, Sausage and Sauerkraut Soup

2 large	Onions, sliced
3 tablespoons	Bacon fat
3 tablespoons	All purpose flour
2 cups	Red wine
1 cup	Vodka
1 (16 oz.) can	Tomato puree
1 teaspoon	Sweet paprika
	Salt and pepper, to taste
2 (1 pound) jars	Sauerkraut
1/2 pound	Sirloin or top round, cooked, cubed
1 1/4 pound	Spicy sausages, cubed
1	Potato, peeled and cubed
1	Apple, peeled and cubed
	Beef Stock

In a skillet, sauté the onions in the bacon fat until just limp. Stir in the flour thoroughly and slowly add the red wine, vodka, tomato puree, paprika, salt and pepper. Cook gently, stirring constantly, until thick. In the slow cooker, alternate layers of sauerkraut with beef, sausages, potato and apple chunks and wine sauce ending with sauerkraut on the top. Add beef stock to just cover. Cover and cook on the low setting for 4-5 hours. If it starts to become dry, add more beef stock.

Notes: This can also be cooked on the stove as well. All of the alcohol cooks out of the wine and vodka leaving a great flavor.

If you want to reduce the fat in this recipe you can use olive oil instead of the bacon fat. Of course you won't have the subtle bacon flavor in the soup.

Beef Taco Bean Soup

2 pounds	Beef rump roast
1 package	Taco seasoning
1 (15 oz.) can	Mexican style diced tomatoes
1 small can	Green chilies
1 (8 oz) can	Tomato sauce
1	Onion, chopped
2 cubes	Beef bouillon
2 (15 oz.) cans	Red kidney beans, rinsed, drained
	Shredded cheddar cheese

Cut the roast into bite sized chunks. Roll them in the taco seasoning and add to the slow cooker. Then add the tomatoes, chilies, tomato sauce, onion, and bouillon cubes. Cover and cook on the low setting 6 hours or until meat is tender.

Add the drained beans and cook until the beans are heated through, about 30 minutes.

Serve topped with cheese, and/or the traditional taco toppings that you like. For a fun dinner, put out bowls of different toppings so everyone can choose their own combination.

Beef and Vegetable Soup
with Yellow Rice

2 pounds	Beef chuck, lean, boneless, cut in cubes
1 large	Onion, thinly sliced
1 cup	Celery, thinly sliced
3 cloves	Garlic, minced
1	Bay leaf
1 large	Red bell pepper, cut into thin strips
1 1/2 cups	Water
2 (14 1/2 oz.) cans	Beef broth
1 large ear	Fresh corn, cut into 3/4" thick slices
4 cups	Cabbage, coarsely shredded
1/3 cups	Cilantro leaves
	Salt and pepper

–YELLOW RICE–

1 tablespoon	Salad oil
1 small	Onion, finely chopped
1 cup	Long grain white rice
1/4 teaspoon	Ground turmeric
1 3/4 cups	Water

The Soup: Arrange the beef cubes slightly apart in a single layer on a shallow baking pan. Bake in a 500 degree oven until well browned (about 20 minutes). Meanwhile, combine the onion, celery, garlic, bay leaf and bell pepper in the slow cooker. Add the browned beef. Pour a little of the water into the baking pan, stirring to dissolve drippings and add to the slow cooker. Add the broth and remaining water. Cover and cook on the low setting for about 8 hours.

Yellow Rice: About 15 minutes before the soup is done, prepare the yellow rice.

Heat the oil in a 2 quart saucepan over medium heat. Add the onion; cook, stirring until the onion is soft but not browned, (3 to 5 minutes). Stir in the rice and turmeric; cook, stirring occasionally, for about 1 minute. Pour in the water and reduce the heat to the low setting and cook until the rice is tender, about 20 minutes.

While the rice is cooking, increase the slow cooker setting to high and add the corn. Cover and cook for 5 minutes. Add the cabbage, cover and cook until the cabbage is bright green, 8 to 10 more minutes. Stir in the cilantro, salt and pepper.

Ladle the soup into wide, shallow bowls and add a scoop of rice to each.

Beer, Cheese and Vegetable Soup

6 medium	Potatoes, peeled and chopped
1 medium	Onion, chopped
1 medium stalk	Celery, chopped
1 medium	Carrot, chopped small
1 clove	Garlic, minced
1/4 teaspoon	Pepper
1 (14 oz.) can	Chicken broth
1 (12 oz.) can	Beer
1 (8 oz.) package	Cheddar cheese, shredded
1/2 cup	Whipping cream

Place the potatoes, onion, celery and carrot into the slow cooker. Add the garlic and pepper and stir to coat the vegetables. Pour in the broth and beer and stir. Cover and cook on the low setting for 6 hours.

15 minutes before you are ready to serve the soup, mash the vegetables with a potato masher. Add the cheese and pour in the whipping cream. Stir until all the cheese has completely melted. Cover and cook an additional 5 to 10 minutes or until hot throughout.

Note: You can use non alcoholic beer if you like. Serve with croutons on top if desired.

Black Bean Soup

2	Onions, chopped
2 cloves	Garlic, minced
3 tablespoons	Butter
1 pound	Black beans, soaked overnight, drained
1	Ham bone, cracked
1 stalk	Celery, chopped
1	Bay leaf
2 quarts	Water
1/2 cup	Sherry or dry white wine
	Salt and pepper, to taste

Sauté the onions and garlic in the butter until transparent. Combine with the beans, ham bone, celery, bay leaf, and water in the slow cooker.

Cook on the high setting for 2 hours, then on the low setting for 8 to 10 hours.

Remove the ham bone and bay leaf. Puree the soup and return it to the slow cooker. Add the sherry, salt and pepper and heat through.

Serve in soup bowls garnished with chopped hard-boiled eggs, parsley, and lemon slices if desired.

Black Bean Soup Mexican Style

2 (15 oz.) cans	Black beans, drained and rinsed
2 (4.5 oz.) cans	Green chilies, chopped
1 (14.5 oz.) can	Mexican stewed tomatoes, with liquid
1 (14.5 oz.) can	Diced tomatoes, with liquid
1 (11-16 oz.) can	Whole kernel corn, drained
4	Green onions, sliced
2-3 tablespoons	Chili powder
1/2 teaspoon	Dried minced garlic
1 teaspoon	Ground cumin (optional)

Combine all of the ingredients in the slow cooker. Cover and cook on the high setting 5 to 6 hours. It can be cooked on the low setting all day if you prefer.

Serve it with shredded cheddar cheese and sour cream.

Broccoli and Potato Soup

4 cups	Water
4 cubes	Chicken bouillon
1/4 cup	Onion, chopped
2 cups	Potatoes, diced
1 bag	Chopped frozen broccoli
2 cans	Cream of chicken soup
1/2-1 pounds	Velveeta cheese, cubed

Mix the water, bouillon cubes, onions, potatoes and broccoli in the slow cooker. Cook on the high setting until the broccoli is thawed. Add the cream of chicken soup and cheese to taste. Cook on the low setting for 2 hours.

Cabbage and Beef Soup

4 slices	Bacon, cooked, crumbled
1 pound	Ground beef, cooked, crumbled
1	Onion, chopped
3	White potatoes, cubed
4 cups	Cabbage, shredded
3 cups	Vegetable broth
1 (28 oz.) can	Diced tomatoes
1 teaspoon	Salt
1/2 teaspoon	Pepper

Place the cooked bacon and ground beef into the slow cooker and stir slightly. Add the onion, potatoes and cabbage. Add the vegetable broth and stir well. Gently stir in the diced tomatoes, salt and pepper. Cover and cook on the low setting for 8 hours.

Cabbage Chili Soup

3 cups	Cabbage, coarsely chopped
1 cup	Onions, chopped
3 cups	Tomato juice
1 (10 1/2 oz.) can	Tomato soup
1 (10 oz.) can	Kidney beans, rinsed and drained
2 teaspoons	Chili seasoning mix

Combine the cabbage, onion, tomato juice and tomato soup in the slow cooker. Add the kidney beans and chili seasoning mix. Mix well to combine. Cover and cook on the low setting for 6 to 8 hours. Mix well before serving.

Cannellini Bean Soup

1 pound	Dried cannellini beans (can use white kidney or white northern if necessary)
6 cups	Water
2	Hot Italian sausages, sliced
1 large	Onion, chopped
1 large	Garlic clove, minced
2 large	Tomatoes, peeled and coarsely chopped
1	Bay leaf, crumbled
1/2 teaspoon	Thyme, crumbled
1/2 teaspoon	Basil, crumbled
3 1" strips	Orange rind
1 teaspoon	Salt
1/4 teaspoon	Pepper
1 teaspoon	Instant beef broth

Pick over the beans and rinse. Cover the beans with water in a large saucepan, bring to a boil, cover and cook for 2 minutes. Remove from the heat and let stand for 1 hour.

In the meantime, brown the sausages in a small skillet. Add the onion and garlic and sauté until soft. Stir in the tomato, bay leaf, thyme, basil, orange strips, salt, pepper and instant beef broth and bring to a boil.

Pour the beans, including any remaining water, into the slow cooker. Stir in the sausage mixture and cover.

Cook on the low setting for 10 hours or on the high setting for 5 hours until the beans are tender.

Cannellini Bean Soup with Penne Pasta

2 (19 oz.) cans	Cannellini beans, drained
1 (1 pound) package	Frozen mixed vegetables
1 (14.5 oz.) can	Diced tomatoes
1/4 teaspoon	Basil
1/4 teaspoon	Garlic
1/4 teaspoon	Oregano
1/2 teaspoon	Salt
1 (12 oz.) bottle	Vegetable juice cocktail
1 cup	Water
1/2 cup	Uncooked penne pasta

Place the beans, mixed vegetables and tomatoes into the slow cooker. Add the basil, garlic, oregano and salt. Pour in the vegetable juice cocktail and water and stir well. Cover and cook on the low setting for 7 1/2 hours.

Stir in the uncooked pasta and increase the heat to the high setting. Cover and cook an additional 20 to 30 minutes or until the pasta is tender.

Note: If you got canned diced tomatoes with the garlic, basil and oregano added you won't need to add any more to your soup.

Cauliflower Soup

1 large	Cauliflower, broken into florets
2 cups	Chicken broth
2 tablespoons	Chicken bouillon granules
2 cups	Half and half
2 cups	Milk
1	Carrot, shredded
1	Bay leaf
1/4 teaspoon	Garlic powder
1/2 cup	Instant mashed potato flakes
1 (8 oz.) package	Cheddar cheese, shredded

Place the cauliflower, broth and bouillon granules into a large soup pot over high heat and bring to a boil. Lower the heat to low, cover and simmer for 25 minutes or until the cauliflower is fork tender.

Remove the cauliflower from the pot and mash with a potato masher. Pour the broth into the slow cooker and add the mashed cauliflower. Add the half and half, milk, carrots, bay leaf and garlic powder. Stir well. Cover the slow cooker and cook on the low setting for 3 hours.

Stir in the potato flakes, cover and continue cooking on low for 40 minutes or until the soup is a thick as you like. Remove the bay leaf.

Place the soup, in batches, into the blender and blend until very smooth. Return the blended soup to the slow cooker, add the cheese and stir well. Cover and continue cooking 15 to 20 minutes or until the cheese has completely melted into the soup.

Note: If you like chunky soups, you can skip the blender step.

Cheese and Broccoli Soup

2 cups	Noodles, cooked
1 (10 oz.) package	Broccoli, frozen chopped, thawed
3 tablespoons	Onions, chopped
2 tablespoons	Butter
1 tablespoon	Flour
2 cups	American cheese, shredded
	Salt to taste
5 1/2 cups	Milk

Combine all of the ingredients in the slow cooker. Stir well. Cook on the low setting for 4 hours.

Chicken Stock

1 (3-4 pound)	Fresh whole chicken, cut into sections
3 quarts	Cold water
2 medium	Onions, sliced
2 stalks	Celery, chopped fine
2 large	Carrots
1 clove	Garlic, crushed
1 teaspoon	Dried thyme or 4 stems fresh thyme
6 stems	Parsley
1 teaspoon	Dried oregano or marjoram
1	Bay leaf
	Salt and pepper, to taste

Place all of the ingredients in the slow cooker. Cover and cook on the low setting overnight.

Before using, carefully remove all of the bones and the bay leaf. If you want a clear broth you can strain it to remove the meat and vegetables to use in another recipe.

Note: This stock can also be made with the leftover carcass of a roasted chicken. The roasting will give it a rich flavor. Be extra careful to remove all of the bones before using as stock.

Chicken Soup

2	Onions, chopped
3	Carrots, sliced
2 stalks	Celery, sliced
2 teaspoons	Salt
1/4 teaspoon	Pepper
1/2 teaspoon	Basil
1/4 teaspoon	Leaf thyme
3 tablespoons	Dry parsley flakes
1 (10 oz.) package	Frozen peas
2 1/2 to 3 pound	Whole chicken
4 cups	Water and/or chicken stock
1 cup	Noodles

Place all of the ingredients in the slow cooker in the order listed, except the noodles. Cover and cook on the low setting 8 to 10 hours, or on the high setting 4 to 6 hours.

One hour before serving, remove the chicken and cool slightly. Remove the meat from the bones and return the meat to the slow cooker. Add the noodles. Turn the temperature to the high setting. Cover and cook 1 hour.

Chicken Soup with Butternut Squash

3 cups	Butternut squash, peeled, cubed
1 (8 oz.) package	Fresh mushroom, sliced
1 cup	Celery, chopped
1 small	Onion, chopped
1 clove	Garlic, minced
6	Chicken thighs, boneless, skinless, and halved
1 cup	Wild rice, partially cooked (optional)
4 cups	Chicken broth
1 teaspoon	Thyme
1 teaspoon	Salt
1/4 teaspoon	Pepper
1/2 cup	Whipping cream
3 tablespoons	Cornstarch

Put the squash, mushrooms, celery, onions and garlic into the slow cooker. Add the chicken thighs on top. Add in the rice and pour in the broth. Add the thyme, salt and pepper and stir well. Cover and cook on the low setting for 6 hours.

Pour the whipping cream into a small bowl. Whisk in the cornstarch until smooth. Stir the cornstarch mixture into the slow cooker. Cover and continue cooking on the high setting an additional 30 minutes.

Note: If you can't find boneless chicken thighs you can use thighs with the bone in. In this case, remove the skin before placing them into the slow cooker and before adding the whipping cream mixture take them out of the slow cooker and remove the bones. Return the meat to the slow cooker with the whipping cream mixture.

This is an author's favorite and the soup pictured on the cover of this book.

Chicken Soup with Mushrooms

1 (10 3/4 oz.) can	Cream of mushroom soup
1/4 cup	Water
4	Chicken breast halves, boneless and skinless cut into cubes
1/2 teaspoon	Salt
1/4 teaspoon	Pepper
1/2 pound	Fresh mushrooms, sliced
1 cup	Baby carrots
2 stalks	Celery, chopped
1/2 teaspoon	Garlic powder

Place the mushroom soup into the slow cooker. Add the water and stir to combine well. Salt and pepper the chicken cubes then add them to the slow cooker. Place the fresh mushrooms, carrots and celery into the mixture. Add the garlic powder and stir well. Cover and cook on the low setting for 7 hours.

Note: If you are a mushroom fan, you can double the amount called for in this recipe.

Chicken Soup with Pearl Barley

1/2 pound	Pearl barley
1 small	Stewing chicken
2	Carrots, cut in chunks
2 stalks	Celery, sliced
2 tablespoon	Parsley, chopped
	Water

Place the barley in the slow cooker and add the stewing chicken. Place the carrots and celery on top of the chicken and sprinkle the parsley over the top. Add enough water to just cover all of the ingredients. Cover and cook on the low setting for 5 hours.

Remove the chicken from the slow cooker. Use forks to remove the chicken meat from the bones. Return the meat to the slow cooker and continue cooking on the low setting for 1 hour or until the barley is soft.

Note: Pearl barley is the barley grain processed by removing the hull and bran. This type of barley is used more often in cooking because it cooks much faster than regular barley. It can be found in most supermarkets.

Chicken Noodle Soup

3	Carrots, peeled, cut into chunks
3 stalks	Celery, cut into chunks
1 large	Onion, quartered
3	Chicken, boneless, skinless breast halves
2 cans	Chicken broth
2-3 cans	Water
1 tablespoon	Dried dill
1 tablespoon	Dried parsley
8 oz.	Noodles

Put the vegetables in the slow cooker. Add the chicken. Pour in the broth and water. (Use the broth cans to measure the water.) Add the dill and parsley. Cover and cook on the low setting for 8 hours.

Remove the vegetables and chicken from the slow cooker. Add the noodles to the broth, turn to the high setting and cook the noodles for about 20 minutes. While the noodles are cooking, shred the chicken and mince the vegetables. Return them to the slow cooker and heat through.

Note: To save time, you can use frozen chicken breasts right out of the freezer if you want.

Chicken Noodle Soup Oriental Style

1 pound	Chicken thighs, boneless, skinless
1 (16 oz.) package	Baby carrots cut in half
1 stalk	Celery, chopped
1 (8 oz.) can	Bamboo shoots, sliced, drained
1 (8 oz.) can	Water chestnuts, sliced, drained
1 (3 oz.) package	Oriental flavored noodle soup mix
1 (32 oz.) can	Chicken broth
1 cup	Frozen sugar snap peas, thawed
2	Green onions, chopped

Place the chicken thighs into the bottom of the slow cooker. Layer on top the carrots, celery, bamboo shoots and water chestnuts in that order. Sprinkle the oriental seasoning packet from the noodle soup package on top, reserving the noodles for later. Pour in the broth but do not stir. Cover and cook on the low setting for 7 to 8 hours.

Remove the chicken from the slow cooker and carefully shred it with two forks. Return the chicken to the slow cooker and stir to combine. Add the noodles from the soup mix into the mixture breaking them apart. Add the snap peas, cover and continue cooking an additional 15 minutes or until the noodles are tender. Sprinkle the green onion on top just before serving.

Note: You can substitute 3/4 cup of regular sweet peas in place of the frozen peas.

Clam Chowder

4 cans	Cream of potato soup
4 cans	New England clam chowder
2 cans	Minced clams, with juice
1	Onion, chopped
1 stick	Butter
1 quart	Half and half

Sauté the onions in the butter, then add all of the ingredients into the slow cooker. Cook on the low setting for 4 hours or until ready to serve.

Clam Chowder with Bacon

4 (6 1/2 oz.) cans	Clams
1/2 pound	Bacon, diced
1 large	Onion, chopped
6-8 large	Potatoes, pared, cubed
3 cups	Water
3 1/2 teaspoon	Salt
1/4 teaspoon	Pepper
4 cups	Milk or half and half
3-4 tablespoons	Cornstarch

Cut the clams into bite sized pieces if necessary. In a skillet, sauté the bacon and onion until golden brown and drain. Put them into the slow cooker with the clams. Add all of the remaining ingredients, except the milk. Cover and cook on the high setting for 3 to 4 hours or until the potatoes are tender.

During the last hour of cooking, combine 1 cup of milk with the cornstarch. Add that and the remaining milk to the slow cooker, stir well and heat through.

Clam Chowder with Vegetables

2 (6 1/2 oz.) cans	Minced clams
2 cups	Potatoes, peeled, cut into 1/2" cubes
1 cup	Onion, finely chopped
1 cup	Celery, chopped
1 teaspoon	Sugar
1/4 teaspoon	Salt
1/4 teaspoon	Pepper
2 (10 3/4 oz.) cans	Condensed cream of potato soup
2 cups	Water
1 cup	Nonfat dry milk powder
1/3 cup	Flour
1 cup	Cold water
4 slices	Bacon, crisp-cooked, drained, crumbled
	Paprika

Drain the clams, reserving the liquid. Store the clams in the refrigerator until later. Combine the clam liquid, potatoes, onion, celery, carrot, sugar, salt, and pepper in the slow cooker. Stir in the potato soup and water. Cover and cook on the low setting for 8 to 10 hours or on the high setting for 4 to 5 hours.

In a medium bowl combine the nonfat dry milk powder and flour. Gradually whisk in the cold water. Stir into the soup. Cover and cook on the high setting for 10 to 15 minutes or until thickened.

Stir in the clams. Cover and cook 5 minutes more. Serve with crumbled bacon and paprika sprinkled on the top.

Corn Chowder

2 (16 oz) cans	Whole kernel corn, drained
2 to 3 medium	Potatoes, chopped
1	Onion, chopped
1/2 teaspoon	Salt
	Pepper to taste
2 cups	Chicken broth
2 cups	Milk
1/4 cup	Butter or margarine

Combine the first 6 ingredients in the slow cooker. Cover and cook on the low setting for 7 to 9 hours. Puree in a blender or food processor, if desired, then return to the slow cooker. Stir in the milk and butter and cook on the high setting about 1 hour more.

Corn Chowder with Bacon

6 slices	Bacon, diced
1/2 cup	Onion, chopped
2 cups	Potatoes, peeled, diced
2 (10 oz.) packages	Frozen whole kernel corn
1 (16 oz.) can	Cream style corn
1 tablespoon	Sugar
1 teaspoon	Worcestershire sauce
1 teaspoon	Seasoned salt
1/4 teaspoon	Pepper
1 cup	Water

In a skillet, fry the bacon until crisp; remove and reserve. Add the onion and potatoes to the bacon drippings and sauté for about 5 minutes; drain well. Combine all of the ingredients in the slow cooker and stir well. Cover and cook on the low setting for 4 to 7 hours.

Corn and Tuna Chowder

1 (10 3/4 oz.) can	Condensed cream of celery soup
1 (10 3/4 oz.) can	Condensed potato soup
2 tablespoons	Pimientos, chopped
1 (8 oz.) bottle	Clam juice
1 teaspoon	Dried parsley
1 (12-15 oz.) can	Whole kernel corn, drained
1 tablespoon	Dried onion
2 (5-6 oz.) cans	Tuna, drained
1 cup	Light cream or half-and-half
	Salt and pepper, to taste

Place the soups, pimiento, clam juice, parsley, corn, and onion in the slow cooker. Cover and cook on the low setting for 4 to 5 hours. Add the tuna, cream, and salt and pepper, to taste. Cook for 1 more hour, or until hot.

Crab Soup

2 cups	Crabmeat, flaked
2 cups	Milk
2 cups	Half and half
3 tablespoons	Butter
2 strips	Lemon peel
1/4 teaspoon	Ground nutmeg
	Salt and pepper to taste
2 tablespoons	Dry sherry
1/2 cup	Saltine crackers, crushed

Place all of the ingredients except the sherry and crackers in the slow cooker. Stir to blend well. Cover and cook on the low setting for 3 to 5 hours.

Just before serving, stir in the sherry and crushed crackers to thicken the soup.

Note: If you'd like, you can add cooked shrimp about 30 minutes before serving.

Cream of Broccoli Soup

2 1/2 pounds	Fresh broccoli, chopped
1 tablespoon	Unsalted margarine
	Water
2 cups	Milk
1/2 cup	Light processed cheese, cubed

Place the chopped broccoli into the slow cooker. Add the margarine on top and fill the slow cooker with just enough water to cover the broccoli pieces. Cover and cook on the high setting for 2 hours.

Pour in the milk, cover and continue cooking for 30 minutes. Stir in the cheese, cover and continue cooking for 20 minutes or until the cheese has completely melted into the soup.

Note: If you'd like some meat in the soup, dice some cooked ham and add it to slow cooker at the same time you add the broccoli.

Cream of Sweet Potato Soup

3	Sweet potatoes, peeled and sliced
2 cups	Chicken bouillon
1 teaspoon	Sugar
1/8 teaspoon	Ground cloves
1/8 teaspoon	Nutmeg
	Salt to taste
1 1/2 cups	Light cream, half-and-half, or milk

Put the sweet potatoes and bouillon in the slow cooker. Cover and cook on the high setting for 2 to 3 hours or until the potatoes are tender. Remove the potatoes and liquid and puree them in a blender. Put them back in the slow cooker with the remaining ingredients. Cover and cook on the high setting for 1 to 2 hours. Serve hot or chilled with a teaspoon of sour cream on top if desired.

Dried Fruit Soup

1 (6 oz.) package	Mixed dried fruit or 1 1/2 cups of the dried fruit of your choice
1/2 cup	Raisins
1 small can	Pineapple chunks with juice
1 large	Granny Smith apple, coarsely chopped
3 cups	Apple or orange juice
1 tablespoon	Lemon juice
1	Cinnamon stick, broken up
2-3	Whole cloves
1/2 teaspoon	Powdered ginger
1 cup	Water

Place all of the ingredients into the slow cooker and mix well. Cover and cook on the low setting for 7 to 9 hours. Before serving, remove the cloves and cinnamon stick pieces and add other frozen or canned fruits, if desired.

Dumpling Soup

1 pound	Steak, lean, cut into 1" cubes
1 package	Onion soup mix
6 cups	Hot water
2	Carrots, peeled and shredded
1 stalk	Celery, finely chopped
1	Tomato, peeled and chopped
1 cup	Packaged biscuit mix
6 tablespoon	Milk
1 tablespoon	Parsley, finely chopped

Add the steak to the slow cooker and sprinkle with dry onion soup mix. Pour the hot water over the seasoned steak. Stir in the carrots, celery and tomato. Cover and cook on the low setting for 4 to 6 hours or until the meat is tender.

In a small bowl, combine the biscuit mix and parsley. Stir in the milk with a fork until the mixture is moistened. Drop the dumpling mixture into the slow cooker with a teaspoon. Cover and cook on high setting for about 30 minutes.

Egg Drop Soup

2 (14 1/2 oz.) cans	Chicken broth
1 quart	Water
2 tablespoons	Fish sauce
1/4 teaspoon	Salt
4 tablespoons	Cornstarch
1 cup	Cold water
2	Eggs, beaten
1	Scallion, chopped
1/4 teaspoon	Pepper

Pour the chicken broth and water into a large saucepan and place over medium heat. Stir in the fish sauce and salt and bring the mixture to a boil.

Whisk the cornstarch and the cold water together in a bowl until smooth. Stir the mixture into the soup. Continue stirring continuously until the soup boils again.

Turn off the heat and remove the sauce pan from the stove. Add the beaten eggs to the soup mixture but do not stir. Pull a fork through the soup. Pour the mixture into the slow cooker. Add the scallions and pepper. Cover and cook on the low setting for 1 hour.

Green Pepper Soup

1 pound	Ground turkey
1 cup	Onion, chopped
1 teaspoon	Fresh garlic, minced
1 (28 oz.) can	Diced tomatoes, including juice
1 (6 oz. can)	Tomato paste
4 cups	Chicken broth
3 cups	Green pepper, chopped
2/3 cup	Rice, partially cooked
2 tablespoons	Brown sugar
1 teaspoon	Dried basil
1/4 teaspoon	Ground cinnamon
	Ground black pepper to taste

In a large skillet over medium heat, brown the turkey, onion and garlic. Drain and place in the slow cooker. Add the rest of the ingredients and stir to mix well. Cook on the low setting for 8 to 9 hours.

Note: If you prefer a thinner soup, add additional water or broth.

Ground Beef and Salsa Soup

1 pound	Ground beef, extra lean
4 cups	Water
1 pound	Potatoes, peeled and chopped
1 medium	Onion, chopped
2 small	Carrots, chopped
2 (4 oz.) cans	Mushroom stems and pieces, drained
1 envelope	Dry onion soup mix
1 (16 oz.) jar	Chunky salsa

Cook the meat in a skillet over medium heat for 12 minutes or until completely browned. Drain well.

Pour all of the water into the slow cooker. Add the cooked ground beef, potatoes, onion, carrots and mushrooms. Sprinkle the dry onion soup mix on top and stir in the salsa. Mix well. Cover and cook on the low setting for 8 hours.

Note: You can substitute ground turkey, chicken or pork if you prefer.

Lentil and Ham Soup

2 cups	Lentils
1 to 1 1/2 cups	Ham, diced
1 cup	Onion, chopped
1	Bay leaf
2 ribs	Celery, chopped
1/2 cup	Carrots, diced
1 clove	Garlic, minced
2 quarts	Water
	Seasoned salt and pepper, to taste

Combine all of the ingredients in the slow cooker and stir well. Cover and cook on the low setting for 8 to 10 hours. Taste and adjust seasonings if necessary before serving.

Lentil and Lamb Soup

1 large	Onion, chopped
1 clove	Garlic, minced
3 tablespoons	Olive oil
4 cups	Swiss chard, spinach, or escarole, chopped
2 cups	Lentils
2	Lamb shanks
1 1/2 teaspoons	Salt
1/2 teaspoon	Ground black pepper
7 cups	Beef broth
1/4 cup	Fresh lemon juice

In a small skillet, sauté the onion and garlic in the oil until tender. Combine them in the slow cooker with all of the other ingredients except the lemon juice. Cover and cook on the low setting for 8 to 10 hours. Add the lemon juice, adjust seasonings if necessary, and serve.

Note: The lamb shanks can be served on the side or the meat can be removed from the bones, diced and returned to the soup.

Lentil and Sweet Potato Soup

1 tablespoon	Canola or olive oil
1 large	Yellow onion, finely diced
2 ribs	Celery, finely diced
1	Red pepper, finely diced
1 large	Sweet potato, cut into cubes
2 tablespoons	Fresh garlic, minced
1 tablespoon	Cumin
1 tablespoon	Salt
1 tablespoon	Ground black pepper
1 teaspoon	Onion powder
1 teaspoon	Oregano
1 teaspoon	Cayenne pepper
1 cup	Lentils
1/2 cup	Quinoa
6 cups	Vegetable stock

Place all of the ingredients in the slow cooker and stir well. Cover and cook on the low setting for 6 hours, or until the lentils and potatoes are soft.

Lentil and Zucchini Soup

2-3 pounds	Beef soup bones
3 medium	Potatoes, diced
1 cup	Onion, chopped
1 (28 oz.) can	Diced tomatoes
5 cubes	Beef bouillon
1/4 cup	Fresh basil, chopped or 2 teaspoons dried
1 teaspoon	Salt
3	Carrots, chopped
2 small	Turnips, diced
3 stalks	Celery, sliced
5 cups	Water
1/2 pound	Lentils
1/4 teaspoon	Pepper
2 medium	Zucchini, chopped

Put everything except the zucchini in the slow cooker. Cover and cook on the low setting for 8 to 9 hours.

Remove the beef bones and cut the meat off. Return the meat to the slow cooker and add the zucchini. Cook on the high setting for 1 hour or until zucchini is tender.

This soup freezes well.

Lima Bean Soup

2 cups	Dried lima beans
8 cups	Cold water
1 cup	Onion, chopped
1	Carrot, peeled and sliced
2 cloves	Garlic, crushed
1 cube	Vegetable bouillon
2 tablespoons	Corn oil
1/2 cup	Onion, finely diced
2 teaspoons	Salt (optional)
	Ground black pepper, to taste

Soak the lima beans in the cold water overnight. Drain them and rinse thoroughly. Place them in the slow cooker with the fresh water, chopped onion, carrot, garlic and bouillon cube. Cover and cook on the low setting for 18 to 24 hours, until the beans are very tender.

Before serving, heat the oil in a small skillet and sauté the finely diced onion until brown. Stir them into the soup and heat for a few minutes.

Note: If you like a smoother soup you can puree it in a blender and put it back in the slow cooker before adding the browned onions.

Meatball Soup

1 package	Fresh baby carrots
1 pound	Small red potatoes, quartered
1 (4.5 oz.) jar	Sliced mushrooms, drained
1	Onion, cut into wedges
1 (18 oz.) package	Frozen, cooked meatballs
1 (12 oz.) jar	Beef gravy
1 (14.5 oz.) can	Diced tomatoes, including juice
1/4 teaspoon	Pepper

Put the carrots into the slow cooker. Add the potatoes and mushrooms on top. Layer the onion wedges on top and add the meatballs. Pour the jar of gravy over the top. Add in the tomatoes including the juice. Sprinkle with the pepper. Do not stir.

Cover the slow cooker and cook on the low setting for 9 hours or until the carrots are tender. Stir to combine the ingredients just before serving.

Meatball and Cheese Soup

2 cups	Water
1 cup	Whole kernel corn
1 cup	Potato, chopped
1 cup	Celery, chopped
1/2 cup	Carrot, sliced
1/2 cup	Onion, chopped
2 cubes	Beef bouillon
1 (16 oz.) jar	Cheez Whiz
–MEATBALLS–	
1 pound	Ground beef
1/4 cup	Bread crumbs
1 large	Egg
1/2 teaspoon	Salt
1/2 teaspoon	Tabasco sauce

Meatballs: Mix the ingredients together thoroughly. Shape into medium size meatballs.

Place the uncooked meatballs and all of the other ingredients, except the Cheez Whiz in the slow cooker. Stir gently. Cover and cook on the low setting for 8 to 10 hours.

Before serving add the Cheez Whiz, stirring gently until well blended.

Minestrone Soup

1 pound	Ground beef
1	Onion, chopped
1 tablespoon	Canola oil
1 (19 oz.) can	Minestrone soup
1 (15 oz.) can	Pinto beans, rinsed, drained well
1 (14.5 oz.) can	Stewed tomatoes
1 (11 oz.) can	Whole kernel corn
1 (4 oz.) can	Green chilies, chopped
1 teaspoon	Salt
1/2 teaspoon	Garlic powder
1/2 teaspoon	Onion powder

In a skillet over medium heat brown the ground beef and onions in the oil, about 12 minutes or until the meat is completely browned. Drain well. Place the meat and onions into the slow cooker. Pour in the minestrone soup, pinto beans, tomatoes, corn and chilies. Add the salt, garlic and onion powder and stir well from the bottom up. Cover and cook on the low heat setting 6 hours.

Note: If you'd like, experiment by adding a few other ingredients such as canned green beans, peas or carrots. See what you can create!

Onion Soup with Mozzarella French Bread

4 cups	Beef broth
1/4 cup	Butter
3 cups	Onion, sliced
1 teaspoon	Salt
1 tablespoon	Sugar
2 tablespoons	Flour
1/4 cup	Dry Vermouth
1 loaf	French bread, cut into slices
1 cup	Mozzarella cheese, shredded

Pour the beef broth into the slow cooker and cover. Set the slow cooker on the high setting and allow the broth to cook while preparing the onions.

Melt the butter in a small skillet over medium heat. Add the onions and sauté for 15 minutes. Stir in the salt and sugar and continue cooking about 5 minutes or until the onions are golden brown. Stir in the flour, mixing well. Place the cooked onions into the broth. Pour in the dry Vermouth and stir well. Cover and cook on the high setting for 3 hours.

When the soup is ready to serve, fill oven proof bowls about 2/3 full with the soup. Turn on the broiler and allow it to heat up. Place a slice of the bread onto the top of each bowl of soup. Sprinkle the bread slice with the cheese. Place the bowls on a baking sheet and place them in broiler just long enough for the cheese to melt.

Pepperoni and Sausage Pizza Soup

1 pound	Italian sausage
1/2 cup	Onion, chopped
2 cloves	Garlic, minced
1 (4 oz.) package	Pepperoni slices
1 (16 oz.) can	Dark red kidney beans, rinsed and drained
1 (16 oz.) can	Light red kidney beans, rinsed and drained
1 (14.5 oz.) can	Dried tomatoes
1 (4 oz.) can	Green chilies, chopped
4 teaspoons	Chili powder
1/2 teaspoon	Salt
1/8 teaspoon	Pepper
1 (15 oz.) can	Pizza sauce

Brown the sausage, onion and garlic in a skillet over medium heat for about 8 minutes. Drain well and place into the slow cooker. Add the pepperoni, both cans of kidney beans, tomatoes and green chilies. Sprinkle in the chili powder, salt and pepper. Pour the pizza sauce over the top and stir well. Cover and cook on the low setting for 6 hours.

Note: This is a great recipe for teenagers. You can chop the pepperoni into small pieces if you prefer. Serve it with an Italian blend shredded cheese sprinkled on top.

Pork Soup

6 medium	Potatoes, quartered
2	Apples, cut into small pieces
1 medium	Onion, diced
1 pound	Baby carrots
2 pounds	Pork tenderloin, cut into large pieces
1 (14 oz.) can	Chicken broth
1 teaspoon	Thyme
1 teaspoon	Garlic powder
1/2 teaspoon	Ground clove
1/2 teaspoon	Ground mustard
1 teaspoon	Salt, to taste
1/2 teaspoon	Pepper

Place the potatoes, apples, onions and carrots in the slow cooker. Add the pork on top and pour in the chicken broth. Sprinkle the spices on top. Do not stir. Cover and cook on the high setting for 4 to 5 hours or on the low setting for 8 hours.

Note: Don't cut the pork pieces too small or it will be too dry.

Pork and Noodle Soup

3 cups	Chicken broth
1/4 cup	Soy sauce
1/4 cup	Dry sherry
3 tablespoons	Light brown sugar
4 cloves	Fresh garlic, peeled and diced
1 2" piece	Fresh ginger, peeled and diced
2 pieces	Star Anise (do not substitute anise)
3 pounds	Boneless pork shoulder
1 head	Bok Choy, roughly chopped
3 1/2 oz	Dried rice vermicelli noodles
1/2 cup	Fresh cilantro, chopped

In a large saucepan heat the chicken broth, soy sauce, sherry, brown sugar, garlic, ginger, and star anise to a rolling boil.

Place the pork shoulder in the slow cooker. Carefully pour the boiling broth over the pork. Cover and cook on the high setting for 3 hours.

Remove the pork from the slow cooker and shred it. Return it to the slow cooker and add the Bok Choy. Cover and cook for an additional 20 minutes.

About 10 minutes before serving, break the noodles in half and place them in a large mixing bowl. Pour about 4 cups of boiling water over them to cook until al dente, about 10 minutes.

Divide the cooked noodles among six soup bowls and ladle the soup on top. Sprinkle with the cilantro and serve immediately.

Pork and Vegetable Soup

1-1 1/2 pounds	Pork shoulder roast, boneless and cut into pieces
1/8 teaspoon	Salt
1/8 + 1/4 teaspoon	Pepper, divided
1 tablespoon	Canola oil
8 small	Red potatoes, unpeeled, quartered
2 cups	Baby carrots, cut in half
1 (12 oz.) jar	Pork gravy
2 tablespoons	Ketchup
1/2 teaspoon	Dried rosemary
1/8 teaspoon	Ground sage
1 1/2 cups	Frozen cut green beans, thawed

Season the pork pieces with the salt and 1/8 teaspoon of pepper and brown them in the oil in a skillet on medium heat. Place the cooked pork into the slow cooker. Add the potatoes and carrots and pour in the gravy and ketchup. Add the rosemary, sage and the remaining pepper and stir well. Cover and cook on the low setting for 7 hours.

Add the green beans and stir to combine. Cover and continue cooking on the high setting for 20 to 30 minutes or until the green beans are tender.

Note: The ketchup gives this soup a rich color and slightly sweet taste. If you don't have time to brown the pork, you can just put it in the slow cooker as is and allow it to brown on its own. Be sure it's fully cooked before serving.

Potato Soup

6-8	Potatoes, cut in chunks
2 medium	Carrots, cubed
2 stalks	Celery, cubed
1 medium	Onion, chopped
1 tablespoon	Parsley flakes
5 cups	Water
	Salt and pepper to taste
1 can	Evaporated milk

Place all of the ingredients except the evaporated mile in the slow cooker and cook on the low setting for 8 hours or until the vegetables are done. One hour before serving, add the evaporated milk and heat thoroughly.

Potato Soup Chilled

5-6 medium	Potatoes, peeled, diced
4	Leeks, thinly sliced
1 cup	Onion, chopped
2 cups	Chicken broth
2 cups	Milk
1 cup	Heavy cream
1 1/2 teaspoons	Salt
	Chives, chopped

Place the potatoes, leeks, onion, and chicken broth in the slow cooker. Cover and cook on the high setting for 2 1/2 to 3 hours or until the vegetables are tender.

Remove them from the slow cooker and puree in a blender and return. Stir in the milk and cream. Cover and cook on the high setting for about 1 hour. Chill completely and serve with chopped chives.

Note: If you prefer a thinner soup you can add more milk or cream as desired.

Potato and Leek Soup

4 cups	Potatoes, diced
3-4 cups	Leeks, thinly sliced
1 bunch	Green onions, chopped
2 cups	Chicken broth
4-6 slices	Bacon, cooked, drained, and crumbled
1 cup	Evaporated milk
1/2-1 cup	Cheese, shredded (optional)
	Salt and pepper to taste

Place all of the ingredients except the milk and cheese in the slow cooker and cook on the low setting for 8 to 10 hours. In the last 30 minutes add the milk and cheese.

Note: For a thicker soup, mash it with a potato masher before serving. Or you can puree it in a blender for a smoother soup. Add additional milk or broth if necessary to get the thickness you prefer.

Pumpkin Soup with Wild Rice

2 cups	White or yellow onion, chopped
2 (15 oz.) cans	Canned pumpkin (not pie filling)
3 1/2 cups	Cold water
4 cups	Chicken broth
1 teaspoon	Ground cumin
1 teaspoon	Dried oregano
1 teaspoon	Light brown sugar
2 (15 oz.) cans	White beans, rinsed and drained
3/4 cup	Uncooked long grain and wild rice
2 teaspoons	Cooking sherry, optional
1/2 cup	Light cream or half and half
1/4 cup	Dried parsley

Place all of the ingredients except the cream and parsley in the slow cooker. Cover and cook on the high setting for 3 1/2 hours or on the low setting for 7 hours.

Ten minutes before serving, stir in the cream, cover and heat thoroughly. Sprinkle with dried parsley before serving.

Rice and Mushroom Soup

1 pound	Whole mushrooms, halved
1/2 cup	Wild rice, partially cooked
1 stalk	Celery, chopped
2	Carrots, chopped
1 (1.8 oz.) envelope	Onion mushroom soup mix
1 tablespoon	Sugar
1 cup	Water
1 (32 oz.) can	Beef broth
1 cup	Frozen sweet peas, thawed

Layer the ingredients in the slow cooker in the order listed.
Pour the water and broth over the top of the ingredients. Do not
stir. Cover and cook on the low setting for 7 hours.

Stir in the thawed peas. Cover and continue cooking on low for
15 minutes or until the peas are tender.

Note: This soup can be frozen for up to 6 months. Be sure to
use air tight containers.

Sausage Soup

1/2 pound	Italian pork sausage
1 cup	Carrots, sliced
1 large	Baking potato, peeled and cubed
1 clove	Garlic, minced
2 (14 oz.) cans	Beef broth
1 (15 oz.) can	Chickpeas, drained
1 (14.5 oz.) can	Tomatoes, including the juice
1 1/2 cups	Water
1/2 teaspoon	Italian seasoning
1	Bay leaf
1 cup	Zucchini, cut julienne style
1/2 cup	Parmesan cheese, grated

In a skillet, brown the sausage in oil over medium heat about 7 minutes or until no longer pink. Drain well and place it into the bottom of the slow cooker. Add the carrots, potato and garlic. Pour in the beef broth and stir to mix well. Add in the chickpeas, tomatoes (including the juice), water, Italian seasoning and bay leaf. Stir again well. Cover and cook on the low setting for 8 1/2 hours.

Remove the bay leaf and stir in the zucchini. Cover and continue cooking 25 minutes or until the zucchini is tender. Sprinkle Parmesan cheese on top just before serving.

Seafood Chowder

2 pounds	Frozen fish filets
1/4 pound	Bacon or salt pork, diced
1 medium	Onion, chopped
4 medium	Potatoes, peeled and cubed
2 cups	Water
1 1/2 teaspoons	Salt
1/4 teaspoon	Pepper
1 can	Evaporated milk

Thaw the frozen fish in the refrigerator. Cut into bite-sized pieces. In a skillet, sauté the bacon or salt pork and onion until the meat is cooked and the onion is golden. Drain and put into the slow cooker with the fish pieces. Add the potatoes, water, salt and pepper. Cover and cook on low setting for 6 to 9 hours.

Add the evaporated milk during last hour. If the chowder is thicker than you like, add more of any kind of milk.

Seafood and White Fish Soup

2 cups	Onions, chopped
2 stalks	Celery, chopped fine
5 cloves	Garlic, minced
1 (28 oz.) can	Tomatoes, diced
1 (8 oz.) bottle	Clam juice
1/2 cup	Water
1 tablespoon	Red wine vinegar
1 tablespoon	Olive oil
2 1/2 teaspoons	Dried Italian seasoning
1/4 teaspoon	Sugar
1/4 teaspoon	Red pepper flakes, crushed
1	Bay leaf
1 pound	White fish, cut into 1" pieces
3/4 pound medium	Uncooked shrimp, shelled, deveined with tails removed
1 (6 1/2 oz.) can	Chopped clams with juice
1 (6 oz.) can	Crabmeat, drained
1/4 cup	Fresh parsley, chopped

Place the onions, celery, garlic and tomatoes into the slow cooker. Pour in the clam juice, water, vinegar and oil. Add the Italian seasoning, sugar and pepper flakes. Stir the mixture well. Add the bay leaf and stir again. Cover and cook on the high setting for 4 hours.

Add the fish, shrimp, clams with juice and crabmeat to the slow cooker. Cover and continue cooking on the low setting for 45 minutes or until the fish flakes easily with a fork. Remove the bay leaf and garnish the top of each serving with the parsley.

Split Pea Soup

1 (16 oz.) package	Dried green split peas, rinsed
1	Hambone, or 2 meaty ham hocks, or 2 cups diced ham
3	Carrots, peeled and sliced
1 medium	Onion, chopped
2 stalks	Celery plus leaves, chopped
1-2 cloves	Garlic, minced
1	Bay leaf
1/4 cup	Fresh parsley, chopped (optional)
1 tablespoon	Seasoned salt (or to taste)
1/2 teaspoon	Pepper
1 1/2 quarts	Hot water

Layer the ingredients in the slow cooker, pour in the water. Do not stir. Cover and cook on the high setting for 4 to 5 hours or on the low setting for 8 to 10 hours until the peas are very soft and the ham falls off bone. Remove the bones and bay leaf. Serve with croutons on top.

Note: This soup freezes well.

Steak Soup

1 tablespoon	Olive oil
1 1/2 pounds	Beef flank steak, cut into cubes
1	Onion, chopped
5 small	Carrots, sliced thin
4 cups	Cabbage, shredded
4	Red potatoes, diced
2 stalks	Celery, diced
2 (14.5 oz.) cans	Diced tomatoes, including the juice
2 (14.5 oz.) cans	Beef broth
1 (10 3/4 oz.) can	Tomato soup
1 tablespoon	Sugar
2 teaspoons	Italian seasoning
1 teaspoon	Parsley flakes

In a skillet, brown the steak cubes and onion in the olive oil over medium heat for about 8 minutes. Drain well. Transfer to the slow cooker. Add the carrots, cabbage, potatoes and celery. Stir in the tomatoes (including the juice) and add the beef broth and the tomato soup. Sprinkle in the sugar, Italian seasoning and parsley flakes. Stir until all the ingredients are combined well. Cover and cook on the low setting for 8 to 9 hours making sure the meat and vegetables are tender before serving.

Note: Any steak will work, including leftover roast. Canned or frozen vegetables can be substituted for the fresh vegetables if you prefer. If you used canned, be sure to check it as it cooks so it doesn't get over cooked.

Sweet Potato Soup

1 tablespoon	Olive oil
2 cloves	Garlic, chopped
1 medium	Red onion, diced
2 small	Jalapeno peppers, seeded and finely chopped
1 large	Yellow bell pepper, finely chopped
1 small	Red bell pepper, finely chopped
1 small	Green bell pepper, finely chopped
2 medium	Carrots, peeled and chopped
2 cups	Butternut squash, peeled and chopped
1 large	Sweet potato, peeled and chopped
2 cups	Vegetable broth
1 (28 oz.) can	Diced tomatoes with juice
1 (15 oz.) can	Pinto beans, drained and rinsed
1/2 teaspoon	Ground cumin
1 teaspoon	Chili powder
1 teaspoon	Salt, to taste
1/2 teaspoon	Ground black pepper, to taste
	Fresh cilantro, chopped, optional
	Sour cream, optional

Place the olive oil in the bottom of the slow cooker. Add the garlic and stir to coat. Add the rest of the ingredients. Cover and cook on the low setting for 5 hours or until the squash and sweet potatoes are soft. Serve with sour cream and cilantro on top if desired.

Note: As is, this is a vegetarian soup. If you would like to add meat, you can add sausage, chicken pieces or beef pieces with the rest of the ingredients. If you use raw meat, you may need to adjust the cooking time.

Sweet and Sour Beef Soup

1 1/2 pound	Beef stew meat
1 (16 oz.) package	Frozen stew vegetables
2 (10 3/4 oz.) cans	Beefy mushroom soup
1/2 cup	Sweet and sour sauce
1/2 cup	Water

Trim the stew meat and cut it into 1 1/2" pieces if necessary. Place the meat into the slow cooker. Place the vegetables on top and stir in the sweet and sour sauce and mushroom soup. Pour in the water and mix together to combine. Cover and cook on the low setting for 10 hours or on the high setting for 5 hours.

Note: You can substitute golden mushroom soup for the beefy mushroom soup if it's easier to find at your store. If you like a thinner soup, add 1/2 cup of beef broth with the water.

This is another author's favorite!

Taco Hominy Soup

1 pound	Ground chuck
2 (15 oz.) cans	Seasoned tomato sauce
1 (15 oz.) can	Diced tomatoes
1 (15 oz.) can	Chili beans with sauce
1 (15 oz.) can	Hominy with liquid
1 (1.25 oz.) envelope	Taco seasoning

Brown the ground chuck in a large skillet over medium heat. Drain well and crumble into bite size chunks. Place the drained meat into the slow cooker. Add the tomato sauce, diced tomatoes and beans stirring to combine. Add in the hominy and liquid, the taco seasoning and stir well. Cover and cook on the low setting for 5 hours.

Note: If you don't care for hominy or can't find it, whole kernel corn will work well too.

Turkey, Potato and Spinach Soup

4-6 medium	Potatoes, diced
1/2 cup	Onion, chopped
1 cup	Smoked turkey breast or ham, chopped
4 cups	Chicken broth
1 teaspoon	Dry mustard
1/2 teaspoon	Salt
	Pepper, to taste
1 (10 oz.) package	Frozen spinach, thawed and squeezed dry
1 cup	Cheddar cheese, shredded, optional

Place the potatoes, onion, turkey or ham, chicken broth, mustard, and salt and pepper in the slow cooker. Cover and cook on the low setting for 7 to 8 hours, or until potatoes are tender.

Add spinach and continue cooking on the high setting for 15 to 20 minutes.

Serve with shredded Cheddar cheese sprinkled on top, if desired.

Turkey Vegetable Soup
with Herb Dumplings

1	Turkey carcass, broken up
8 cups	Water
4 cubes	Chicken bouillon
1 (10 oz.) can	Diced tomatoes
1 stalk	Celery, diced
1	Carrot, diced
1	Turnip, peeled and diced
1	Onion, diced
4 teaspoons	Dried parsley (divided)
1	Bay leaf
1 1/2 cups	Flour
2 teaspoons	Baking powder
3/4 teaspoon	Salt
1/2 teaspoon	Dried rosemary
3 tablespoons	Solid shortening (Crisco)
3/4 cup	Milk

Place the turkey carcass into the slow cooker and pour the water over top. Add the bouillon cubes. Add the diced tomatoes, celery, carrot, turnip and onion. Add 2 teaspoons of the dried parsley and the bay leaf. Cover and cook on the low setting 7 hours.

Remove the turkey carcass out of the soup being sure you get all of the small bones. Remove the meat from the bones and return the meat to the slow cooker.

Put the flour, baking powder, salt, rosemary and remaining parsley into a bowl. Cut in the shortening with a pastry cutter or two knives until the mixture becomes coarse. Add enough of the milk to the flour mixture to moisten it but leaving the mixture thick enough to make mounds on the end of a spoon. Drop the mixture by spoonfuls into the slow cooker. Cover and cook on the high setting for 20 minutes.

Note: To save some time you could use packaged biscuit mix.

Vegetable Soup

2 (14.5 oz.) cans	Diced tomatoes with green chili peppers
1 (15 oz.) can	Kidney beans, rinsed and drained
1 (15 oz.) can	Chickpeas, rinsed and drained
1 (10 oz.) package	Frozen corn
1 cup	Onion, diced
2 (8 oz.) can	Tomato sauce
1 (1 1/4 oz.) envelope	Chili seasoning mix
1 cup	Water

Pour the tomatoes (including juice) into the slow cooker. Add the kidney beans, chickpeas, frozen corn and onion. Add the tomato sauce and stir until well combined. Add the envelope of seasoning mix and water and stir well. Cover and cook on the low setting for 6 hours.

Vegetable Beef Soup

1 pound	Ground chuck
1 cup	Onion, chopped
1 cup	Celery, chopped
1 (28 oz.) can	Whole tomatoes, chopped
3 cups	Potatoes, diced
1 (16 oz.) can	Cut green beans
2 teaspoons	Chili powder
2-3 dashes	Cayenne pepper sauce
2 (10 1/2 oz.) cans	Condensed beef bouillon
1 cup	Carrots, sliced
1 teaspoon	Salt
1 teaspoon	Worcestershire sauce
1-2 cups	Water

In a skillet, brown the meat, onions and celery; drain off fat. Add to the slow cooker and stir in the remaining ingredients. Cover and cook on the low setting for 8 to 10 hours.

Winter Squash Soup

2 (10 oz.) packages	Frozen winter squash puree
1 cup	Chicken broth
1 cup	Onion, chopped
1/8 teaspoon	Ground black pepper
1/2 teaspoon	Salt
1/2 teaspoon	Dried thyme
1/4 teaspoon	Dried sage
3/4 cup	Heavy cream
	Sliced green onions, sour cream, or chopped fresh parsley

Place the frozen squash, chicken broth, onion, and seasonings in the slow cooker. Cover and cook on the low setting for 4 to 5 hours. Add the cream and continue cooking for 15 minutes.

If desired, remove from the slow cooker and process in a blender until smooth. Serve with a garnish of sliced green onions, sour cream, or chopped fresh parsley.

Note: If you can't find frozen winter squash puree in your store, you can substitute 2 and 1/2 cups of cooked and mashed winter squash.

Zucchini and Bell Pepper Soup

1	Onion, chopped
2 cloves	Garlic, minced
1 (4.5 oz.) jar	Sliced mushrooms, drained
1 (14.5 oz.) can	Chicken or vegetable broth
1/4 teaspoon	Salt
1 large	Zucchini, sliced
1 small	Red bell pepper, cut into strips
1 small	Yellow bell pepper, cut into strips
1 teaspoon	Italian seasoning
1 (14.5 oz.) can	Diced tomatoes with Italian herbs

Place the onion, garlic and mushrooms into the slow cooker. Pour in the chicken broth, add the salt and stir well. Cover and cook on the low setting for 10 hours.

Stir in the zucchini, bell pepper strips and Italian seasoning. Pour in the diced tomatoes (including the juice) and stir well. Cover and continue cooking on the high setting 30 minutes or until the zucchini is fork tender.

About the Author

Cathy L. Kidd is a craftsperson at heart. For as long as she can remember she has been creating things with her hands. She has done crochet (taught to her by her Aunt Carol), stained glass (learned by taking a class), candlemaking (learned from an ebook and experimenting) and homemade bread making first by hand and then with the use of a bread machine (learned initially with the help of Betty Crocker!)

Her first two books, *Homemade Bread Recipes – A Simple and Easy Bread Machine Cookbook* and *How to Make Homemade Bread – Simple and Easy Bread Making Tips and Recipes* came out of her enjoyment of homemade bread making.

For this book she pulled out her old slow cooker to make soup. Homemade soup is the perfect pairing for homemade bread so it made sense that it would be her next book. So put on your slow cooker and bread machine in the morning and you'll have a simple and easy meal ready at dinner time!

Her other books include:
- How to Make Homemade Ice Cream: Simple and Easy Ice Cream Maker Recipes
- How to Make Smoothies: Simple, Easy and Healthy Blender Recipes
- Dehydrating Food: Simple and Easy Dehydrator Recipes

For more recipes visit:
> www.easyhomemadebreadrecipes.com

And join us on Facebook at:
> www.facebook.com/RecipesForYourKitchenAppliances

CPSIA information can be obtained
at www.ICGtesting.com
Printed in the USA
LVHW081746261219
641750LV00011B/1235/P

9 781630 229580